LAKES AND RIVERS

A Freshwater Web of Life

Philip Johansson

Enslow Elementary
an imprint of
Enslow Publishers, Inc.
40 Industrial Road
Box 398
Berkeley Heights, NJ 07922
USA

http://www.enslow.com

Enslow Elementary, an imprint of Enslow Publishers, Inc.

Enslow Elementary® is a registered trademark of Enslow Publishers, Inc.

Library of Congress Cataloging-in-Publication Data

Johansson, Philip.
   Lakes and rivers : a freshwater web of life / Philip Johansson.
      p. cm. — (Wonderful water biomes)
   Summary: "Presents information on the biome of lakes and rivers following the food web and
      flow of energy from sun to plants and animals"—Provided by publisher.
   ISBN-13: 978-0-7660-2812-8
   ISBN-10: 0-7660-2812-7
   1. Freshwater ecology—Juvenile literature. I. Title.
   QH541.5.F7J64 2007
   577.6—dc22   2006100470

Printed in the United States of America

10 9 8 7 6 5 4 3 2

To Our Readers: We have done our best to make sure all Internet Addresses in this book were active
and appropriate when we went to press. However, the author and the publisher have no control over
and assume no liability for the material available on those Internet sites or on other Web sites they may
link to. Any comments or suggestions can be sent by e-mail to comments@enslow.com or to the
address on the back cover.

Photo Credits: © 1999, Artville, LLC, p. 8; Hemera Technologies, Inc., p. 2; Photograph taken on
Earthwatch Institute "Lakes of the Rift Valley" program, pp. 5, 6, 7; Photo Researchers, Inc.: A. Cosmos
Blank, p. 39, Altitude, p. 13, Andrew Syred, pp. 21 (water bear), 35, Edward Kinsman, p. 36 (top), E.R.
Degginger, pp. 21 (coontail), 27, Farley Lewis, p. 15, Gary Meszaros, pp. 19, 22 (tadpole), p. 41 (top),
Nature's Images, pp. 21 (suckers), 22 (suckers), 36 (bottom), Dr. Nick Kurzenko, p. 25, Novosti Press
Agency, p. 11, Rod Planck, pp. 16 (duckweed), 29, Ron Sanford, p. 38, Simon Fraser, p. 28, Steve
Maslowski, p. 20, Wayne Scherr, p. 31, WorldSat International, Inc., p. 12; Photos.com, pp. 18, 21
(cattails, egret, beaver), 22 (cattails, egret), 32, 37, 41, 43; Shutterstock, pp. 9, 16, 21 (duck), 23,
26, 44.

Illustration Credits: Copyright © 1987, 1998 by Dover Publications, Inc.

Cover Photos: (clockwise from upper left) Photos.com, Shutterstock, Shutterstock, Farley
Lewis/Photo Researchers, Inc.

Dr. David Harper is a scientist at University of Leicester, England. He studies the ecology of Lake
Naivasha and other Rift Valley lakes in Kenya, East Africa. The volunteers depicted in Chapter 1 are
from Earthwatch Institute, a nonprofit organization. Earthwatch supports field science and
conservation through the participation of the public. See www.earthwatch.org for more information.

Table of
CONTENTS

Chapter 1

A WORLD of WATER

As his motorboat passes a hidden cove on a lake, Dr. David Harper points out a group of hippos floating in the shallow water. A majestic African fish eagle swoops over the boat to land on a floating piece of driftwood. Other birds call from trees on the shore. The day is hot, and the air over the lake is moist.

Dr. Harper and his team of three assistants are studying the plants and animals of Lake Naivasha,

Kenya's second-largest freshwater lake. Like many parts of Africa, the lake is a great place to find wildlife. But the team is looking for something that doesn't belong in the lake.

"Here's where we'll start," says Dr. Harper. He turns off the motor and the boat drifts to a stop near the lake's edge. The team jumps out and begins wading in a line. They use long-handled nets to rake the lake bottom in search of small animals there.

Dr. David Harper's assistants search for unusual wildlife in Kenya's Lake Naivasha.

Crayfish were brought to Lake Naivasha from the United States in the 1960s to provide food for Kenya's growing population.

Before long, an assistant calls out, "Got one!" She shows her net to Dr. Harper. He confirms that she has caught a Louisiana crayfish. The small, lobsterlike animal is thousands of miles, and an ocean away, from Louisiana.

Freshwater Food

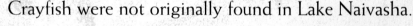

"To most of you, hippos and giraffes are exotic species," says Dr. Harper, who scoops the crayfish out of the net and puts it in the boat. "But here in Kenya, these crayfish are the exotic ones."

Crayfish were not originally found in Lake Naivasha. They were brought there in the 1960s as a food source for Kenya's growing population. The crayfish needed food too, and they ate the plants that naturally grew on the bottom of the lake. These lake plants were not adapted to these new, hungry plant eaters. After forty years, the crayfish

had removed most of the kinds of plants that once grew in the lake.

The team finds a dozen more crayfish in the next hour. Then they gather at the boat to measure the crawling animals, mark them, and return them to the water. They also count and identify plants growing on the muddy bottom. They collect samples of the water, which includes floating algae and tiny animals. All this information will help Dr. Harper and other scientists

Lake Naivasha is Kenya's second-largest freshwater lake. Dr. Harper and other scientists are studying how the food web in the lake has been affected by changes in the environment.

understand how the crayfish has changed the food web in Lake Naivasha.

Water, Water, Everywhere

Although nearly three quarters of the earth's surface is covered with water, most of that is salty ocean water. Only 3 percent is freshwater. Three quarters of that freshwater is frozen solid in ice and glaciers. Nearly another quarter is underground. That leaves less than one percent of the world's freshwater for lakes, rivers, ponds, and streams. It seems like just a drop, but this freshwater is what makes life on land possible.

Lakes and rivers are important to people, but they are also home to many unique plants and animals, from duckweed to otters. Scientists like Dr. David Harper are working to understand how plants and animals live together in freshwater biomes.

AFRICA

Kenya

AFRICA

WHAT IS A BIOME?

Lakes and rivers are one kind of biome. A biome is a large region of the earth where certain plants and animals live. They survive there because they are well suited to the environment found in that area.

Each biome has plants that may not grow in other biomes. Soil, water, rocks, and climate all help to determine the kinds of plants that grow there. Cattails grow in marshes, but not in forests. Tall trees grow in forests, but not in deserts. The animals that eat these plants help form the living communities of a biome. Exploring biomes is a good way to start understanding how these communities work. In this book you will learn about lakes and rivers and the plants and animals that live there.

Chapter 2

The
FRESHWATER
BIOME

Lakes and rivers can be found all around the world, from the Arctic tundra to the tropical rain forest. They can be small, quiet ponds or raging rivers that flow over waterfalls. They come in all sizes and shapes, depending on the shape of the land and the climate. The only things needed are a source of freshwater and a low area in the land to hold the water.

This water can come from rain, melting snow and ice, or springs that release it from underground.

Lake Baikal, in Russia, holds more water than any other lake on Earth. It measures 600 kilometers (372 miles) long, and covers an area about the same size as the state of Maryland. It is deeper than a mile, and holds one fifth of the world's surface water. Another fifth is contained in the Great Lakes of North America, the largest group of freshwater lakes in the world. Of course there are thousands and thousands of smaller lakes, and even smaller ponds, around the world.

Lake Baikal in Russia is the largest lake in the world. It contains about one fifth of the world's total freshwater.

The Great Lakes of North America are shown on this map. These five lakes contain one fifth of the world's freshwater.

Rivers are different: They are on the move. The Amazon River in South America has the greatest amount of water of any river. It carries water about 6,300 kilometers (4,000 miles) from the Andes Mountains to the Atlantic Ocean. That's as far as from Florida to Alaska. The Mississippi River runs 3,765 kilometers (2,340 miles), from the Midwestern United States to the Gulf of Mexico. Smaller rivers and streams spill into these large rivers along the way.

Together, all the lakes, ponds, rivers, and streams make up the freshwater on the surface of our planet. Like a network of life-giving blood, these bodies of water bring Earth's plants and animals a constant supply of important freshwater.

Standing Still

Lakes are usually more than two meters (six feet) deep. This is deep enough for fish and other freshwater life to survive year round. They can even live through very cold winters because the water on the bottom does not freeze. Ponds are smaller and may have water in them for only part of the year. Some lakes and ponds actually have salty water in

The Amazon River in South America is almost 4,000 miles long.

them, like Utah's Great Salt Lake, but this book will focus on freshwater ones.

The temperature of lakes and ponds depends on their location, their size, and the season of the year. They can range from 32°F (0°C), or frozen, to balmy temperatures of 80°F (27°C) or more. Big, deep lakes tend to be colder than small, shallow ponds, because the sun has a harder time warming them up. Even so, a big lake in the Tropics, such as Lake Naivasha, would be warmer than a small pond in the Canadian winter.

On the Move

Rivers and smaller streams contain freshwater that is always on the move. They flow downhill with the help of gravity. Rivers usually start in the mountains, where they are fed by rain, melting snow, lakes, or water from underground. Eventually, rivers flow into the ocean or another waterway. Over long periods of time, flowing rivers can carve deep

valleys and canyons in the land. They do this
through the process of erosion, the wearing away
of the earth as the water flows over it. Rivers carry
tons of dirt, sand, and gravel downhill and drop
them when they slow down near the sea.

Rivers change as they flow downstream. Imagine
following a river from the smallest trickle in the
mountains to a sweeping bay in the ocean. You
would pass by steep brooks, raging rapids, gently
sloping streams, meandering marshes, and nearly

The Colorado
River carves a
valley through
the colorful rock
layers of Dead
Horse Point
State Park, Utah.

motionless water closer to the sea. Water near the beginning is clearer, cooler, and has more oxygen than water near the river's end. These different conditions attract different kinds of plants and animals. The life of a river is always changing as it crosses the land, making it an exciting place to explore.

✓ **All around:** Lakes and rivers are found nearly everywhere in the world, from the Arctic to the Tropics.

✓ **Deep enough:** Lakes are bodies of water deep enough for plants and animals to live there year-round.

FRESHWATER FACTS

✓ **Going with the flow:** Rivers run downhill with gravity, bringing snowmelt or rainfall to oceans.

✓ **River of change:** As rivers flow downstream, their water changes. It gets warmer, cloudier, and lower in oxygen.

LAKE AND RIVER COMMUNITIES

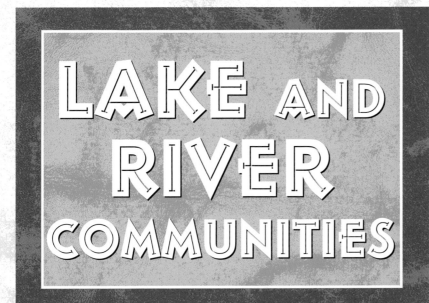

Like biomes on land,

lakes and rivers are made up of communities of plants and animals. Communities are the groups of living things found together in a place. Each living thing has a role in the community. Some plants and animals depend on others for survival.

Cattails are one plant in the lake and river food web.

Energy Flow in a Lake or River

Freshwater plants, such as cattails, trap the sun's energy for their food. They use the energy to make sugars from water and carbon dioxide (a gas in the air and dissolved in the water). They store the sugars and use the energy later when they need it to grow.

Some animals have to eat plants to get their energy. Animals that eat only plants are called herbivores. Tadpoles and snails are examples of herbivores. Animals that eat other animals to get their energy are called carnivores. Smallmouth bass, otters, and great blue herons are carnivores. Some animals, such as raccoons, eat both plants and animals. They are called omnivores.

In lakes and rivers, another source of food is all around. These are plankton, tiny plants and animals that float through the water for any animal to snap up. Like larger animals, plankton animals eat plankton plants to get their energy. Some lake and river animals eat plankton from the water for their food. They include fish called shad as well as mosquito larvae.

Other animals get their energy from dead plants and animals. Particles of dead plant and animal material

◇ 19 ◇

Largemouth bass are carnivores. They eat other animals.

are called detritus. Some animals can break down detritus in the bottom of lakes and rivers. They capture nutrients from detritus so that it can be recycled through the food chain. Small crustaceans, bottom-feeding fish like suckers, worms called nematodes, and other detritivores do this job.

The Food Web

The flow of energy through lakes and rivers from the sun to plants to herbivores to carnivores and detritivores follows a pattern called a food web.

SOME PLANTS AND ANIMALS IN THE
LAKE AND RIVER FOOD WEB

PLANTS

Eaten by

Willows

Cattails

Rushes

Reeds

Sedges

Pondweeds

Cow lilies

Duckweed

Milfoil

Water celery

Coontail

Algae

Plankton plants

HERBIVORES

Eaten by

Beavers

Beetles

Leaf miners

Caterpillers

Ducks

Midge larvae

Caddis fly larvae

Minnows

 Moose

Tadpoles

Snails

Copepods

Water bears

Water fleas

Rotifers

Plankton animals

CARNIVORES

Frogs

Salamanders

Dragonfly larvae

Otters

Trout

Bass

Sunfish

Perch

Egrets

Herons

Kingfishers

Eagles

Catfish

Minnows

ETRITIVORES

Nematodes

Suckers

Copepods

SUNLIGHT

USED
BY

PLANTS 〜〜〜 HEAT LOSS

EATEN
BY

HERBIVORES 〜〜〜 HEAT LOSS

EATEN
BY

CARNIVORES 〜〜〜 HEAT LOSS

DETRITIVORES
eat dead plants and animals

Like a spider's web, it is a complicated network of who eats whom. The web connects all the plants and animals of a freshwater community. For instance, tadpoles eat algae. Bass, in turn, eat tadpoles. Bald eagles eat bass. When eagles die, crayfish and worms eat them.

Together, plants and animals pass energy through the lake and river community. They also use some of the energy to live. At each stage of the food web, some energy is lost as the animals use it. It is also lost in the form of heat. More energy from the sun has to be trapped by plants to keep the community alive.

By looking at the plants and animals of rivers and lakes, you will see how they may rely on one another. If you take any plant or animal away, it could change how the community works.

Chapter 4

LAKE AND RIVER PLANTS

When most people think of plants, they picture common flowers or trees that grow on land. But there are also many plants that grow in water. These are called aquatic plants. Some of them are familiar, some are not, and some are even hard to see. Together, aquatic plants provide oxygen, food, and hiding places for the animals of lakes and rivers.

◇ 24 ◇

Three Ways to the Sun

Although aquatic plants live in water, they still rely on the sun to grow. Water plants have three basic ways to reach that life-giving light. Some plants are rooted underwater but stand up, or emerge, out of the water. These are called emergents. They include many familiar plants, like cattails and irises,

Irises are rooted under the water and bloom above the surface. They are called emergents because they emerge, or stick up, above the water.

*W*ater lilies are a type of floating plant. They are rooted under the water and have floating leaves that trap the sun's energy.

as well as unusual ones like the papyrus that grows in Lake Naivasha.

The leaves of the second group, floating plants, are full of air. They float on the water's surface in the full sun. Many of them, such as water lilies with their showy floating flowers, are rooted in the mud below. In the Amazon River, there is a giant water lily with leaves big enough to hold a small child out of the water. Other floating plants, like tiny duckweed or tropical water hyacinths, have roots that simply hang in the water.

A third group of aquatic plants, called submergents, are harder to find. They grow completely beneath the surface of the water. They often have soft, feathery or narrow leaves that wave in the water. Some submergent plants found in lakes and rivers include milfoil, coontail, and eelgrass.

Coontail is a plant that lives completely under the water. It has soft leaves that can wave in the water without being damaged.

Another type of submergent plant is hard to see without a microscope. These tiny plants, called algae, are so simple that many scientists do not even consider them true plants. They do not have stems and roots like other plants. Despite their size, algae are a very important food for lake and river plant eaters. They grow on the surface of rocks and larger plants or float in the water. If you've ever slipped on a slimy streamside rock, you've probably found a colony of algae.

Green algae provide food for many animals in the freshwater biome. Hairlike green algae hang from these rocks.

On the Water

Near the edge of a lake, the water is shallow. Emergent plants such as rushes, reeds, and sedges stick out of the water. They are rooted firmly in the muddy or sandy bottom. Pickerelweed has heart-shaped leaves with spikes of purple flowers. Arrowhead is named for the shape of its leaves. Often just one type of emergent plant, like cattails or papyrus, takes over whole areas.

Deeper water is too deep for emergent plants to stand up. Instead, floating plants and submergent plants grow. Pondweeds and cow lilies float on the surface. Milfoil waves in the water below. In even deeper water, the sun cannot reach submergent plants, and roots of floating plants cannot reach the lake bottom. There the most common plants are ones with no roots at all. Duckweed has tiny, round leaves that float on the surface. Microscopic floating algae live near the water's surface.

A frog peeks out from a lake that is covered in duckweed.

Many of the same plants that are found in lakes and ponds can be found in rivers as well. The difference with rivers is that the water is always moving, so floating plants would not do well there. Rivers tend to have more strongly-rooted submergent plants. Beds of water celery wave in the current like fields of grass. In the fastest streams, as they cascade down over rocks and rapids, the only plant life that can survive are algae clinging to the stones.

On the Edge

Lakes and rivers have other plants that don't grow in the water but are still important to life there. These are plants that grow right on the edge of the water. Mosses cling to riverside rocks. Grasses and sedges wave in the breezes from the water. Larger plants like sheep laurel and willow stretch over the water to reach the most sun. Trees such as hemlock and silver maple thrive in the abundant moisture and sun at the water's edge.

Many different plants can grow along the edges of lakes and rivers. This is the Snake River in Idaho.

Land plants provide many benefits to the life of lakes and rivers. They prevent erosion of the shore, and therefore keep the water clean. Some aquatic animals, such as beavers and muskrats, find food and shelter among shoreline plants. Others, such as trout, rely on overhanging trees to provide shade. Without shade, river temperatures may get too warm for the insect food they need to survive. Trees growing by the water also eventually die and fall into the water, creating places for fish, turtles, and other animals to live. In streams, fallen trees create the pools in which trout and other fish live.

*Fallen trees in
lakes and rivers
create shelter
for fish and
other animals.*

LAKE AND RIVER PLANTS

✓ Wet diversity: Lakes and rivers have many different kinds of plant forms, including emergent plants, floating plants, and submergent plants.

✓ Plant zones: Different kinds of plants grow in different parts of a lake or pond, according to how deep it is.

✓ Life in the fast lane: Rivers have many of the same plants as lakes, but they have more well-rooted submergents. Fast streams have few plants other than algae.

✓ Tiny plants: Microscopic algae grow on the surface of rocks and float in the water, providing abundant food for aquatic life.

✓ Life on the edge: Shoreline plants provide protection from erosion, along with food, shelter, and shade for lake and river animals.

Chapter 5

LAKE AND RIVER ANIMALS

The **plants** found in lakes and rivers give food and shelter for many animals, from tiny insects to soaring eagles. Some of them, like salmon, need the cool water and high-oxygen levels of rushing streams. Others, such as carp or catfish, prefer the warm, still waters found in lakes.

◆ 34 ◆

Many birds and mammals can be found in or near rivers and lakes. They include river otters, beavers, great blue herons, kingfishers, and raccoons.

Plant Eaters

The tiniest plant eaters in lakes and rivers are among the most important. Plankton animals—too small to see without a microscope—float in the sunny water. They eat floating plankton plants. Some plankton animals are water bears, water fleas, and rotifers. There are also tiny, floating animals related to crabs and lobsters, called copepods. This kind of herbivore in turn is food for many larger animals.

On the edges of lakes and rivers, algae grow on the surface of rocks and plants. Snails and tadpoles eat these algae. Insects such as beetles, leaf miners, and caterpillars chew on larger plants that grow above the water. Many insect larvae eat plants underwater.

Water bears are microscopic plankton animals. They eat plankton plants. They are also food for other, larger animals.

Some fish eat algae and other aquatic plants. These include minnows and related fish called suckers. They scrape the layer of algae off of rocks and plants. The Asian grass carp, which can grow to a size of 50 pounds, can eat large amounts of submergent plants.

Beavers, muskrats, and nutrias are mammals that eat plants in and around lakes and streams. They find

Diving beetles eat small fish and minnows.

The razorback sucker has become endangered in the Colorado River. They scrape algae off of rocks to eat.

most of their food on the edge of the water. They eat branches and bark from trees growing there. Beavers also build dams from these same branches, changing parts of streams into ponds. Some birds eat plants on lakes and rivers. Ducks, geese, and swans eat duckweed. They also dip their head underwater to find submergent plants.

Beavers are herbivores. They use tree branches found along the edges of rivers as a food source. Beavers use the same tree branches to build dams.

A bull moose eats grasses that grow below the surface of this lake in Alaska.

Other large herbivores come to lakes and rivers just to eat. Moose visit lakes to eat the soft plants growing just under the surface. In Africa, waterbuck graze on the lush grass that grows around lakes. Hippos eat the same grass during the night, but they spend the hot days resting in the water.

Animal Eaters

The many snails, insects, and tiny crustaceans in lakes and rivers are food for a variety of small

predators there. Dragonfly larvae float on the water surface, preying on smaller insects and fish that go past them. Frogs, salamanders, and turtles eat insects near the edge of the water.

Some fish, like trout, gulp large insects floating on the surface of the water. Others, like minnows, sunfish, and perch, pick their prey off the surface of plants or rocks. These hunters are especially active at dawn and dusk, when they can sneak up on their

A frog leaps toward its dinner, a black-winged damselfly.

prey. Catfish hunt for tiny fish and crustaceans at night, using their sensitive whiskerlike barbels to find their prey.

Small fish are often eaten by larger fish. Largemouth bass, as their name suggests, use their large mouth to suck in prey they find out in deep water. Pike and gars lurk in thick vegetation. When smaller fish come close enough, the predators dart out and grasp them in their toothy jaws. Other large fish, like the striped bass found in some big rivers, cruise around in schools, snapping up fish and crustaceans in their path.

Birds are also important predators in lakes and rivers. Kingfishers swoop down from nearby branches to snatch up small fish. Herons and egrets stalk through the vegetation on the water's edge to find fish, frogs, and other small animals. Loons can dive up to 200 feet deep and stay underwater for three minutes to catch fish. Eagles and ospreys soar overhead in search of fish near the surface. They grab

A largemouth bass (top) and a kingfisher both eat frogs.

their prey in their talons, then take it to a high nest or branch to eat.

Mammals also join in the feeding fun. Otters spend most of their lives in lakes and rivers, and are able to swim quickly after fish. Raccoons find frogs, crayfish, and other small prey along the water's edge. Bears are famous for fishing for salmon as the fish try to swim upstream to lay eggs.

Wet and Wonderful

Lakes and rivers are important to a variety of plants and animals. Some animals spend their whole lives there, while some, such as moose, just come there for food or shelter. Some animals, like caddis flies and frogs, spend part of their lives underwater, then emerge as adults. The freshwater found in lakes and rivers is also vital to countless other animals that just visit for a drink.

Scientists like Dr. David Harper are working to understand how freshwater food webs work so that

people can try to manage lakes and rivers better. For instance, in Lake Naivasha, crayfish are just one of the many animals that were brought in to the environment. Several exotic fish were also brought there, with the hope of providing more for local fishermen to catch. As a result, all the native fish from the lake are now gone. Changes in the food web can affect the other plants and animals that rely on the lake. Dr. Harper hopes that by learning more about Lake Naivasha, and by teaching local people about it, the lake food web can be saved from further damage.

✓ Tiny floaters: Plankton animals too small to see without a microscope live in the open water, eating plankton plants.

✓ Water babies: Some animals, like dragonflies, caddis flies, midges, and frogs, spend only the first stages of their lives in lakes and rivers.

✓ Wet lunch: Moose and other large mammals often visit lakes and rivers.

LAKE AND RIVER ANIMALS

otter

✓ Crawly food: Insects, snails, and tiny crustaceans are food for many other animals, including dragonfly larvae, frogs, and fish.

✓ Different strokes: Predators hunt in different parts of lakes and rivers, using different techniques. Bass hunt in open water, pike lurk in the shallows, and birds dive down from above.

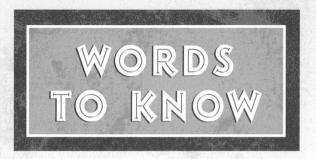

WORDS TO KNOW

biome—An area defined by the kinds of plants and animals that live there.

carnivore—An animal that eats other animals.

climate—The long-term pattern of temperature and rain- and snowfall for a given area.

community—All the plants and animals living and interacting in an area.

crustaceans—Animals with no backbone, a hard shell, and jointed legs, including crabs and their relatives.

detritivore—An animal that eats dead plants and animals.

detritus—Particles of dead plant and animal matter.

emergents—Plants with underwater roots whose stem and leaves stand up out of the water.

erosion—The wearing away of earth by the action of water or wind.

exotic species—A kind of plant or animal that did not originally live in an area.

food web—The transfer of energy from the sun to plants to herbivores to carnivores, and then to detritivores.

habitat—The area in which a certain plant or animal normally lives, eats, and finds shelter.

herbivore—An animal that eats plants.

larvae—The wormlike stage of an insect's life cycle.

nematodes—Tiny, round worms that live in the mud.

nutrients—Chemicals necessary for plants and animals to live.

omnivore—An animal that eats both plants and animals.

plankton—Tiny plants and animals that float in the water.

submergents—Plants that grow beneath the water surface.

LEARN MORE

BOOKS

Beatty, Richard. *Rivers, Lakes, Streams, and Ponds*. Austin, Tex.: Raintree Steck-Vaughn, 2003.

Butterfield, Moira. *Animals in Lakes and Rivers*. Austin, Tex.: Raintree Steck-Vaughn, 2000.

Cherry, Lynne. *A River Ran Wild: An Environmental History*. Orlando, FL: Voyager Books, 2002.

Johnson, Rebecca L. *A Journey Into a Lake*. Minneapolis: Carolrhoda Books, 2004.

———. *A Journey Into a River*. Minneapolis: Carolrhoda Books, 2004.

Toupin, Laurie. *Freshwater Habitats: Life in Freshwater Ecosystems*. London, UK: Franklin Watts, 2005.

INTERNET ADDRESSES

Missouri Botanical Garden. *Freshwater Ecosystems*.
http://www.mbgnet.net/fresh/index.htm

U.S. Environmental Protection Agency. *Clean Lakes*.
http://www.epa.gov/owow/lakes/

Water on the Web. *Lake Ecology Primer*.
http://waterontheweb.org/under/lakeecology/index.html

INDEX